Always sit
away from

## Lardcake

To

Paul

with

thanks,

David McGimpsey

Montreal
April
2001

# LARDCAKE

## POEMS BY DAVID McGIMPSEY

E C W   P R E S S

CANADIAN CATALOGUING IN PUBLICATION DATA
McGimpsey, David, 1962–
Lardcake : poems
ISBN 1-55022-278-3
I. Title.
PS8575.G55L3 1996     C811'.54     C96-930146-4
PR9199.3.M33L3 1996

Back cover photo by John Fraser.

Design and imaging by ECW Type & Art, Oakville, Ontario.
Printed by Imprimerie Quebecor l'Eclaireur, Beauceville, Québec.

Distributed by General Distribution Services,
30 Lesmill Road, Don Mills, Ontario M3B 2T6.

Published by ECW PRESS,
2120 Queen Street East, Suite 200
Toronto, Ontario M4E 1E2.

# Table of Contents

## ONE

## TWO

## THREE

# ACKNOWLEDGEMENTS

I would like to thank John Bennett, April
Bulmer, Jim Crosbie, Lynn Crosbie, John
Fraser, Scott Macdonald, and Karen Massey
for all their generous support and encouragement.
Special thanks to Michael Holmes.
And grateful thanks to all my family, especially
the folks in Ville D'Anjou — my parents John
and Mary McGimpsey, my sister Janice and my
brother Mike.

Some of these poems appeared (or will appear)
in the journals *What*, *Tickle Ace*, *Rampike*, *Zymergy*,
*We Eat This*, *The Apalachee Quarterly*, *Poetry Motel*,
*Matrix*, and in the anthologies *Sounds New* (Muses
Company), *32 Degrees* (DC Books), and *The Last Word*
(Insomniac Press).

To Carol

# ONE

# Corragio, Lumpy

I could tell by the look in her eye
that she had a mild case of hamburger disease
and taking the bus crosstown,
even to see Amy Grant, was out of the question.

There was a lightning storm the other day
and there were tree limbs everywhere.
I was thinking of my life in retail,
what did I care of being struck down?

Alone at the lunchouse
I thought about all the H.S. glamour-pusses
who called me stinky
and mispronounced "Wisconsin" as "Wistonsin."

The cheese was on them, so to speak,
but it was time to get back on the job:
I'm not living in Ratburg anymore,
at least not after this shift, this customer-service.

# Shannen Blazon

The last time she threatened me with a .22
we were on the Santa Monica Freeway,
smelling like rich Los Angeles,
pretending to know the mumbled words in popular songs.
It was before the earthquake,
before she picked up that shake in her voice
most noticeable when she says
"I wasn't fired, I quit."
The barrel of the gun was like candy,
I would've held it for her,
still cocked and aimed,
just in case her arm was getting tired.
The central joke was "faster, faster
we've got to get to the Whisky."
She was all sloppy, like God herself,
out for a spin under the haphazard stars.
She put the thing away and sang:
"Bobbitt-o, Bobbitt-y, boo."

We picked up her friend with the big nostrils
and ended up at the Hotel Mondrian again;
*de stijl*: straight uncut lines.
I just tried to feel grateful.
Her teeth all crooked in the right ways,
her nose all crooked, her eyes . . .
She screamed to a makeshift entourage:
"I'll still be in this business
when Christina Applegate is folding tacos
at some dive in Yorba Linda."
She was oblivious to my heart.
She continued her monologue:
"Jenny's just jealous. That's all.

That was *my* book selling in Chicago
and that was *me*, 'the next Bette Davis'
according to that tv-critic out in the village there.
How could sweet Jenny's pain,
what with all her bellyflops,
just go away?
That girl will never be alright
until she learns to forgive me
for being a better actress."

Smoking, drinking, but never overeating.
Her leather pants always just so.
Her black velvet smock still very 90210.
The man with the nostrils read from his poems,
something "for a friend at Hazelden."
She had nothing she said but recalled for us all
her final task at the Lycée Français,
to translate a favorite movie scene:
"*J'avais pensée que nous whatever au Club Babylon !*"
"*Encore?*"
It was quite impressive, I clapped real loud
and she asked me why I just didn't go home.
I said rough justice was all that I was looking for
not exculpation, not even a promise
to get me in to see her agent.
She gave me $200 and said "get a cab, lady."
The nostril-man laughed.
I said a bunch of things I never said
because I was tired, chastened,
intrigued by the cash.

The Santa Monica Freeway has crumbled now.
The whole city smells like concrete-dust.
I heard the tabloids said it was never meant to be.
They misspelled my name,
but now that's what I go by, professionally.

# Jacko's Wacko Pre-Nups

The King's daughter is in the hotel,
the perfume is everywhere.
In a few hours the staff is instructed to greet her
by her married name.
In silence, they practise it so elegantly
they look like they're blowing smoke-rings.

The self-anointed King of Pop
is on the telephone, holding his nose.
He listens to a lawyer tell an anecdote
involving a ball player and a dozen roses.
The lawyer's voice never wavers,
sounding slow and pre-recorded.
The lawyer goes yes sir, yes sir
without really listening to what is said:
"I keep the chimps, the llamas and the giraffes.
I keep the golf carts named after Motown stars,
the pictures, the awards, the gifts,
the copyright to the overseas re-sale of recordings and
        merchandise . . .
I get to keep my conductor's cap."

She invokes the name of L. Ron Hubbard
to a room service kid late with her bottled-water.
"And God shall have no choice"
went her spiel until the kid was exhausted
and forgot to see how she looked like somebody else.
When the kid was in the hall he exhaled loudly,
cringing up to his neck with the unsaid
and with his new insight into the evils of tipping.
Alone, she tries singing "PYT,"
tries to remember she looks like someone else.
Out the window the streets of Santo Domingo

are hazed-over with summer.
The smell of fried plantains mixes
with exhaust from leaded gasoline
and rises up to the windows
so, so "dangerous to our skin."

He hangs up the telephone,
somebody with the necessary documents
will walk in the room any minute.
It'll all be in the supermarkets in hours.
The buzz of mopeds and scooters,
of tourists saying "Hooup! Wuupo!"
(or whatever it is that they say)
is hurting his head.
"It sounds like being stabbed in Chicago"
he says to the man with the documents
who can barely understand
a thing the client squeaks.

She comes in to sign the papers,
laughing like she's being looked at
by an old boyfriend at the other end of the room.
He says something but it isn't valentining.
She signs dramatically
looping her loops like they've never been looped before,
and says "this one's for the Colonel"
which brings a big laugh,
then an awkward silence.
Downstairs the staff has started to look
at their reflections in the brass railings.

The songs begin to change while the arrangement is assured,
they go:

> Hold me around the waist.
> I wish I was dead.
> Hold me like a teenage dance.
> I wish I was dead.

# Roger Clintonesqueria

In Aphelia House I lunge at my TV-friends
when they say things that let me down;
I'm less demonstrative with real people,
preferring to avoid their meaningful comparisons.

On magazine covers the lips are the thing:
always ready to speak French, to giggle,
to curse even simple bar-pickup good looks —
come to me for a celebrity lawn layout.

Joey Travolta is playing me on the screen
notice how he works in the sleepiness
esp. when he asks "can't you do it for me?
I gave up on myself sometime in the early eighties."

Jett Williams is singing my panegyric medley
the tunes muddied together in a careless mix;
the attitude is 100% State Fair;
almost drowning out the call on the pig-races.

Dom DiMaggio is up at bat again
or is it actually Vince DiMaggio?
It is hard to tell except that it isn't the one
looking sad in the newspapers everyday.

If Don Ho had a brother named Edward
would Ed Ho be as comfortable as Don
working the crowd in the fabulous Luau Room
at the fabulous Waikiki Hilton in Waikiki?

If the lawn started to turn to dirt
would they ask me if I had grazed there too often?
Munch the world away and blame it on my upbringing,
or Ronald Reagan (that would be best of all!)

There's no tragedy in Burgerworld tonight
no woebegotten talent undiscovered;
the world has done its work in forgetting
Jennifer Plath, T.P. Eliot and Dave Joyce.

Through the leaves and through the sky
have to feed the thing and jazzercize.
Down the stairs and down the halls
try to sound as smooth as Pat Summerall.

The magazines will call anybody your cousin,
the President's brother, the President's son.
It won't matter if you think you've seen it all
but it's quite an old and perplexing booby prize.

Huzzahs to Pete Best, Gummo Marx and Frank Stallone
the world is their oyster and their free gumball.
Can't help but hear, really hear, the poetry
from their magazine-article anodynes.

"The difference between you and Gummo Marx
is that I've *heard* of Gummo," she said to me
as I escorted her to a gala premiere
where I sat and dreamed up new cover-songs.

I think they can, I think they can.
The chug of that horrible engine
its cranapple-flavored monoxide asphyxiating me
and asking me for an autograph.

Jim Belushi is my brother
when he puts on his dark glasses and dark suit
and takes on the demanding Chi-town crowd:
puddingheaded twister, blues enough for me.

# Joan Lunden/Alan Thicke Sex

When the Pasadena streets were empty
& the parade routes cleared of trash
we climbed aboard a wilting Rose Bowl float
& made love in a blue & white bower.

Cold for California we kept thinking,
tracing the wrinkles about the eyes
with nervous fingertips; "go slow, go slow"
we said to the drunk driving in the cab.

The stars above us full of lips & arms;
the sidewalks at either side too soft,
like we could roll off & meatball bounce
onto a lawn & celebrate our celebrity thighs.

We will get together in New York City
& address the pure uselessness of May
with hotel sex workaholism;
in the cold we'll talk of our Pasadena thing.

Taking the rose-petals off with our toes,
we covered our stomachs with a damp mulch,
absent of fragrance
& the only thing between us.

We unlatched the platform from the cab
& the cab went on, weaving, oblivious
& the float beached at an intersection
like a maudlin, heavy whale.

We watched the cab putter along;
there go our marriages, better than before,
all towards Los Angeles, fully dressed,
speaking wordlessly of television success.

# The Divine Inspiration of Elvis Presley

*sacre couer*

"Oh, don't kid yourself" she said to me
"You still sound like someone with a graduate degree."
Her friend nodded; she had freckles.
Was that it for me?
I can't remember what I said,
    probably switched subjects
pretended I cared about an anthologizer
    & this horrible University.

Trying to shake
a year-long depression;
new hobbies include birds,
television talk shows,
the history of the state of Texas
& writing about
trying to shake off a year long
    depresso.

I think I hear the right thing
    in Elvis Presley's voice
esp. in "Puppet On a String"
A wee little thing to sing
    to pretty Shelley Fabares
around the swimming pool.

O Elvis,
    true son of God.
Mocked sitcomically
& trashed by State U types
who need eponyms
for all the things they're better than:
instant coffee, processed cheese,
getting fat.

FAT.

Even if I can't forgive myself,
    he can.

# Jurassic Dave

I am the fly in amber
the bug with some blood left.
Listen to this,

the fly,
the thing,
it always turns out to be me;

I was a good kid in creative writing classes
but now I've become a Barbra Streisand type,
singing my name

and of how hard it is to sing my name
on such and such a budget
in this Oscar-snubbing world.

Nothing has fossilized
except my basketball legs
and my preference for Diet Coke.

If it doesn't appeal to narcissism
is it appealing at all?
Extra-value meals and *Cheers* re-runs

are the puddles I jump to drown in.
A million miles down, I listen out of politeness,
my voice doesn't sound like that, does it?

# TWO

# Charlie's Reality

I am a hungry man
I will eat my hand one day
to calm my feelings of failure

& wave my stump like glory
at the beginning of a World Series
game.  I was married,

mummified, we sat around
peering through our well wrapped gauze
our yellowing mortgaged hermitage

& our wedding photos shrunk
into subway booth snaps,
into wallet sized daguerreotypes

that crumbled underneath my pillow
as I continually searched for the cool side
in our poor smoky nights

& divorced to the daylight miraculously
money came in tubs
the color of pistachio ice cream

I fancy myself a mastermind supersleuth
so I buy this agency —
a girls only detective agency

& my cabal solves the worst crimes
they were L.A.P.D. cadets
babes, well disposed to .36 calibre pistols

fingerprint deductions, second guessing
the criminal mind
& foiling villains in bikinis.

"Freeze!" they say in my sleep
maybe one day they'll say
"Charlie was ok" & they'll solve

my murder — the cleaver edge & veins
that seem to be written in the stars
& when they walk away, from behind

from my tinted part of heaven I'll shout
"Catlike, catlike, catlike — I know"
& my angels will find out why

make sure the worms turn the right way
& I am still the villain in my ex's notebooks
now, I can sit & repeat garlic

& hear of their adventures —
I hear they've been abused
in the women's prison

& nowhere near there have I dwelled;
come like a perfect brass crescendo:
Kelly, Sabrina & Jill

# Howard Hears Marion Downstairs

I hear you downstairs in the morning.
Your bones are too big; drumbeating out
the sun with their yearning syncopations.

There will be another kind of birdcage for you
and another yellowed Eisenhower era for me;
I hear you downstairs making plans.

You talk out the window to the lanky
brown haired man with crooked, gapped teeth.
You say something that in the movies

would go like this;
"just because I'm a nun
doesn't mean I can forget I'm a woman."

We quiver like chicken hinds
after the voodoo priest has bitten off the head
and its blood forms icicle drips

at the defiant mouth. We shake
like delirious hands, fumbling with a bottle
of Wild Irish Rose by the cold lakeshore.

I hunger for oatmeal that goes right to the blood
and a Messiah with a body like my own
minus the war in Europe,

minus the years of cheap ice cream,
and the rationalization
"maybe if I turned off my tap of Milwaukee's finest."

You are moving our furniture,
at least that's what it sounds like.
Everything is pushed and pulled with railway chugs.

It could be the sound of you scraping
off faded wallpaper; but ours
is brand new and bright as your hopeful trousseau.

Isn't this just like a bruise?
All the purple and yellow anybody could stand
is down there somewhere

amidst the sound of "shh"
and chair coasters rocking against the floor
like hard waves throwing driftwood at the strand.

# Darrin's Affair

Samantha can levitate make her hair brown
her fingernails green & her body Watusi long
all through the power of witchcraft & love

& I waded into it like a kiddie pool
seemingly refreshing but no place for me
eating purple jello with nutrasweet every night

all the while fidgeting with my tie
thinking what is she going to do next
when will she save my life again

by the power of witchcraft & love
& I walk into the world with a big cumbersome
life preserver that I have to lie to conceal

makes me wish I could have just a little slip
a little rush of clandestine unease & pain
I work in advertising & have secretaries

& these advertising secretaries in business
skirts & sometimes motions of curious flirtation
while Samantha just twitches her nose

turns me into a beast, into Cary Grant
turns me into favorite lovers from past lives
& all I was looking for was a little suburbia

a double martini & middle aged impotence
thoughts of one secretary at work
out for dinner after work & to her apartment

I think she's slim but one day she'll be fat
thoughts of an aging ad man considering a toupée
& my consistent carpediem campaigns

to buy that car or that house right now
& what's the use if you're not willing to risk
everything in a 2 a.m. something gone wrong

it makes me love all the less, wraps my giblets
in saran wrap & tosses the beating part
into the microwave on low heat

dinner is ready for me, another martini
in her apartment & one with Sam when I get home
life is perfect, a marketing strategy

# Chuck Cunningham's Pro Basketball Career

one play in a forgettable gym I'll remember
a deep baseline shot & it just goes over their fingers
& arches into the hoop & they've fallen down

they've lost & the fans thought it was cool
it wasn't my shot but it went in
this wasn't supposed to be my league but it is

professional in Greece for me
headlines in Cyrillic I'll never understand
& my parents in Milwaukee think I'm dead

people come into pop's hardware store
& ask him whatever happened to Chuck
& he hides in the tins of paint & mop sponges

traces the letters of my name in window caulking
& hiring any kid who looks a bit like me
pop is like that but still at dinner no word

4 years at DePaul on scholarship & my body grew
five more inches, well beyond standard casket size
& well beyond anybody's expectations

an endless dramatization of the crucial shot
in empty gyms & mute cheers to myself
loneliness hearing balls bounce on the gym floor

a plangent call to consider something else
sitting on the bench in Phoenix, then in Maine
dying a little more with each insane coach

it is a sweet ridiculous irony playing in Greece
living again the life of an American
jobbing a poetry as simple as ball through hoop

# Kelly Leaves the Charles Townsend Detective Agency

I've been thumbing the book of quotations
trying to find the right way to say fuck you
a way to slam the door like a teenaged Zeus

all silver with precious hurt & insight;
the grease of the bards is used & tasty
& made for situations just like this.

I can't stand the agency anymore
can't bear being a Revlon detective
an angel with a gun for L.A. county

you're either a detective or you're not;
jab a snub-nosed pistol in my ribs
& you'll find out exactly what I mean.

Palm trees, frozen yogurt & roller skates
would be the only fun in town
if I continued these silk pajama jobs,

& it's not that I don't care about my tan
or that I really take pride in this work,
but if you remain one of Charlie's angels

you'll end up as old as Mick Jagger —
an olympian bimbo to a dismayed crowd.
The agency house is brittle with white

& throw pillows & sickly french perfumes
that have lost their original intent
& now smell like basement-dried kidney pulp

oh, those 70s ideas aren't worth two-bits:
those wide legged slacks in bright new fabrics
& hair blow dried into arboreal forms

all as strange as Tantalus's banquet,
when Jill & Sabrina are still kept
by a pale Hefner impersonator on the phone.

My door may say Kelly Garrett, P.I.
& then again it may threaten prosecution
or threaten dog bites that leave carmine sockets

wherever it wishes to chomp down;
I may even grow my wella hair wild
& haunt L.A. like the Eumenides.

There are better ways to resign I'm sure
perhaps some blind, handless oracle
has left a few notes around to copy —

meanwhile, a bit of Venice Beach & I retire
my .36 tucked nicely in the sand
ready for any of life's contingencies.

# Elly May Grows Old

I have grandkids of my own they keep their walkmans on
their skin is bad & under influence of potato chips
they ask "what kind of music do you like Granny Elly?"

with a Tennessee smoker's hack I pretend senility
to scare them away "Varmints! I recall this
here city boy son of a banker he would call on me

& start singing opera, licking my forearm
in the parlor & showing off some acting
& we'd wear dinner clothes & play football"

those kids go off somewhere in the mansion
while their parents sleep it off in the bedrooms
upstairs, they are in Versailles & ready to loaf

I clean a gun in the living room so they think twice
when something rustles them from bed
it's Christmastime soon in Beverly Hills

exhusbands phone & I put them down
with bible quotations & laugh
then assuage them with delicate acts of self pity

yellow pills & murmurs like "it's all over"
my skin is loose & leathery but resilient
like Pa's millions which protect me & I them

this is no dowry & to our investors I scream
"profit profit profit" O Granny, Jethro & Pa
a multitude of lies form the complete me

a soft gavotte step of necessity for survival
when no cancer has claimed me
& when my kids & stepkids wait with drool

what I like to do is take my rifle & shoot
into the orange trees & scare the birds
scare the birds away from me & my home

# The Flying Nun's Vows

Orville & Wilbur Wright are dipped in bronze
because they saw their collection of sticks
make it over a ridge in North Carolina,

but they had nothing as magic
& nothing as boeing as my cornette habit,
blessed by the allmighty's icy voice

giving me the gift of flight:
takes me from the friendly grey confines
of the San Tanco convent to every corner

of every orphanage in sunny Puerto Rico.
Mother Superior cries "Sister
Bertrille, Sister Bertrille! Stop that!

Come down!" her voice like
some far off coyote wounded in the hills.
"If God had intended nuns to fly,

the Pope would be an owl."
God blessed my habit & I can fly,
what can I say?

It may not be part of the rosary call,
but it takes me to the ground
where I can say no to the Carlos a-go-go

& yes to poor Marcello the orphan boy.
There's Hollywood movies about Jesus:
Willem Dafoe, Marjoe Gortner & Charlton Heston, I think.

Who knows what the Son of God had in mind?
I don't know where I stand
& after all, I don't have to stand.

I'll just scoot from rooftop to rooftop
confident that you can sell this nun anything
as long as you call it salvation by a hat.

So, cuddle in the arms of your security guards
& sing your dry jingles of tomorrow's diet
into your tantrum-smashed telephones.

O Carlos, Carlos, your James Bond hips
& Fernando Lamas eyes don't mean Bo Diddley
to my Mother Superior & I.

Believing is some kind of jelly: some believe
in the lyrics to Whitney Houston songs, some believe
Jesus will slip them through the cold sea.

Lord, content the orphans, the Chinese
while I go for a ride in the sky.
My shoes: corrective, flying.

# Edna Loses the Store

she had quit her job to start up the shop
dyed her hair a further shade of orange
until it had a young florescent glow

like velvet paintings of Nevada sun,
it was her turn to grow & sing bluemoon
she always worked out her problems baking

"it's unusual but it works for me"
she says with her bright Wisconsin aplomb
in her famous cheese puffs, tarts & croissants

are these ingredients: a failed marriage
a guitar playing son still on the loaf
& the many trials of the girls she cares for

'Edna's Edibles' is no old bakery
along its wall you'll find onions & caviar
behind the counter there's cornbread & brie

& it all sold like hotcakes with butter
until one evening & that song of no more
that little lapse no bigger than a fly

leaving the heat on a small pan of oil
& turning around to walk to the store
oblivious to that twist of her hand

& when she got back, with 10 lettuce heads
ears still buzzing with Peekskill gossip
the firemen were scooting around, swearing

This is the biggest fire they've ever seen
Peekskill seems as small as an apple
& about as dangerous to safety

there was nothing that they could really do
pretend it's the 4th of July & watch
& Edna drops & cries from the reality

how tender that olive oil looked bottled
she yells way into the Catskill mountains
"my shop! my beautiful shop! o, o girls!"

she wishes it would smell of all the shop's food
gently roasting way into the wind
instead it pours acrid plastic smoke

black as hockey tape, searing her nostrils
with its caustic smell until she chokes hard
she knows it's all over & she coughs again

she knows her policy is outdated
& will not cover it more than a layer
of yellow paint or floral wallpaper

she felt the fire take some orange away
& her hair was emptied into the flames
everybody says "at least you're not hurt

thank god nobody was hurt or killed"
but maybe it would've been better Edna thinks
to join all the angels who've died in fires

# THREE

# In Memoriam: A.H. Jr.

A few weeks before he died
thin, thin from the cancer
Alan Hale was stopped by a teenager
who pumped gas at an L.A. station
& asked the gaunt skipper if he was alright,
if he was dieting or something
like Oprah, Lasorda or some other famous,
formerly overweighted.
"Yes that's right" the mighty sailing man said
"we're doing the series again
& this time I'm going to play Gilligan."
& he drove out into the afternoon.
Now his body is out in the Pacific
mixing with coral reef & Catalina trash,
whole with the universe, taking time out,
resting forever from the question:
who was responsible for the fate of *The Minnow*?

Brave in diagnosis, brave in chemo,
brave in goodbye. From heaven send a message,
have a few hot dogs & smile.

Once, when you were in the greenworld
tempest in the uncharted areas of the sea,
you fell under the terrible curse of Kona.
Digging through the fine island sand,
making practical refrigeration
to store Mary Ann's guava jelly
you unearthed the idol head,
its mouth downturned,
its jagged teeth poised to cut through skin.

The curse of Kona, you said,
(inbetween frantic conjurings of fates
more terrible than being stranded
on an island full of idiots,)
could only be cured by Watumbi's dance.
Only Watumbi's dance,
doctored to the rhythms of the tropical forest,
could deliver release into the world
of the relatively uncursed.
"Superstitions don't have to be ridiculed"
you said to Prof. Roy Hinckly, PhD (TCU)
who was irreverent in answering your call
for the dance but admitted
that he had seen many things
that defy the laws of reason in his years
as a castaway in the cancerous sun.
The Professor tried his best
but couldn't help start dictating all the triumphs
his Cartesian mind had brought them all:
saved them from the deadly Mantis Carni bite
with an antidote of ground clam shells & papaya roots,
saved them from marauding Marubi headhunters
simultaneously translating their intent to kill
& finding a safe, inner-island cave
to huddle & coo about the lost USA;
saved the crew from long-term effects
of radioactive vegetables the size of trees.
The skipper set the Prof. straight, said, "son
it doesn't hurt to believe in the curse of Kona
or believe Jesus Christ is waiting for me, drunk,
on the other side; it doesn't matter tonight if I
send in a subscription for Scientific American,
anyway you have it we are stranded here on this island,
the two foot hole in the Minnow untouched
by doctoral insight — we won't be rescued tonight."

Stupid or no, you ran around the island
through nests of damselflys, crunching
the bambooish undergrowth at your feet,
burning; sweat tracking the folds of your neck,
burning salty-dog neck & chin.
Jonas Grumby,
you ran straight into a palm tree & conked-out.
A severe case of *bumpinus on the nogginus*
but when you came to, you still believed.

You had survived the wreck
of the infamous *USS Indianapolis*;
bobbed helplessly in warm water
American canapes for swarming tiger sharks,
banjo sharks, what you will.
From Guadalcanal with your purple heart
the scars zigzagging around your shoulders
like a complex tattoo of a jungle fire.
Through the years the colors started to dull,
even in the land of Gauguin
is there ever enough tropical variety?
I don't think I can just sit back & hear anymore
not if we must touch bottom of the dolphinless sea.
Dive underneath all the water
five miles deep in the Izu trench off Japan
& tell me what's there if you can.
Weren't you the leader?
There has to be a better government.

I can see the x-ray shadows.
I can see them come back after the triumph
of telling everybody you had it licked.
A shadow on the x-ray screen, a *mass*,
doctors/oncologists yapping before their knives
their cobalt, their interferon,
their understanding
there's a certain point of no return.
How did that storm come in & in 3 hours
sweep you out to sea?
Sweeping you out forever
& making you what you are?
*Salut mes joyeaux naufragés.*
I can see the x-ray shadows.

Monkeys throw plastic explosives overhead.
The rich couple, their money useless
still manage to have a certain
I-paid-my-way-through-Harvard kind of fun.
The Professor will work for them one day.
& Mary Ann will take to the street
to sell her preserves.
You danced with Ginger Grant,
the most beautiful woman in the world.
Her ballgown bared of its sequins,
her red hair drawn back with a beret
of sticky orchids. She rehearsed
lines from a prison movie in your ear.
You danced in the courtyard
in front of the bamboo huts
that lasted for 12 lonely years;
through typhoons, dictators & rock stars.

Japanese lanterns, crepe paper & torches
giving the cleared part of the jungle
a sense of festival & backyard safety.
The coconut-Victrola playing Paris accordion —
the air of the left lagoon bank
soft & warm, protected for the Tiki,
ready for the lost
& ever & always
260 nautical miles SW of Honolulu.

Hours spent, beautiful, swinging imperceptibly
in a navy issue hammock,
the silhouette of your belly on the wall,
candles flickering gently on the green palm fronds,
the captain's hat over your eyes.
Skinny Mulligan, what's-his-face,
above you, ready to fall out & rake hell.
Dreams of Malaysian food, of Australian wine
of sailor stuff from Seattle to Hong Kong.
Dreams of maybe getting married,
of strolling with prams through the San Diego zoo
sort of just like I-don't-know-who.
Hours spent reading the naval manual,
(not one for staring at Manuel's navel)
tying bamboo sticks together,
sharpening bits, things for survival he says
survival enough to kill the time.
No phones, no lights, no microwave.
Hours thinking about the fate of *The Minnow*.
One wrong weather report & that was it.
It happens to everybody in some way.
Did y'all fasten your anchor
when you threw your life overboard?

"When I get back" you prayed
"I'll do my best to clear my name, extend my commission
& still surprise the world by doing something nice
for that stupid kid."
Broadway impressarios could visit the island
as much as they wanted, proposing
a musical Hamlet or a musical Lear —
it didn't help one bit.
You said "I can't remember everything, it gets lost
deep into the bright afternoons.
It's amazing, I stayed fat through it all,
through everything. Isn't that funny?"

The Skipper & Gilligan will be friends forever,
despite their tragic mistakes.
The worst things will still happen,
they always do, despite our bonds.
Things settle in the damp roots of our lungs
in the red fibres of the fibres of our muscles
& rot.
It was a wild time:
sand in everything, amazing inventions.
The sputum of the atoll-gods rippling lagoon water
like spacecraft tumbling back to America.
Don't let go of my hand because I'm dying
of cancer or drowning in the Irish sea.
Brave it out & bury nothing, let it drift
with everything still wet & alive.
Let it drift aimless,
just another tour gone astray.
Christmases, rainy seasons, mosquitoes,
all forgotten, just like last February
in the suburbs.

*Ces après-midis disparaissent*
*et Gilligan et le Capitaine goûteraient*
*leurs tartes aux crème d'ananas*
*avec nous-autres.* Goodbye little buddy.


Victrola dancing Ginger accordian lighted
ricewine crepe-paper Ginger perfume
jungle Paris redhaired moonlit Ginger.
You survive, not to cry
like Pagliacci,
but because life holds to you so well.
You wore your captain's hat proudly
receiving visitors to your family-restaurant:
*The Skipper's Lobster Barrel*
on La Cienga Blvd. in Los Angeles, California.


Dozing through a little busride
through the birch forests of Upper Canada
the tinge of diesel seeping in the luxury coach.
The view out into the stretch of winter,
faded trees scratching the horizon,
squaring out the meagre farmland.
Nothing there that wasn't frozen.
In the dark February plain
the voice of the seven stranded castaways
deep in the Boreal forest
"Skipper! Professor!"
I thought I heard somebody cry.
"I think the Howells have scurvy!"
Saying it was only a TV show
is like saying it was only a friend,
only my brother, only my father.

Put the antennae high, pay your cable bills.
To volcanoes fresh & lagoons anew.
He was like to ponder expeditious rescue.
He'd say "when I get back to civilization
I'll tell you exactly what I'm going to do:
I'm going to have a tall glass of cold beer
& I won't spill a drop.
I'm going to order a steak, New York cut,
medium rare & two inches thick."
How thick? "Two inches thick!"
In the plate will rest the slightest residue:
blood, spice & fat
agents of flavor after the meat is gone.

# Babe Ruth In Love

Babe Ruth, Yankee slugger extraordinaire,
Red Sox lefty who never lost a World Series game,
neck tumor / throat cancer victim
victor over millions of hot dogs & beers
is just another who didn't really die.
Friends, he just excused himself from the hospital bed,
too scrawny for pinstripes,
his face drooping, badly ravaged,
& wandered out under the weary stars
& went somewhere altogether Ruthian
& picked himself up a brontosaurus bone.
He had a few & gnawed away the prehistoric gristle
till his teeth were as sharp as the Spanish blade
& the dinosaur bone was fashioned,
alla Bambino, into some kind of Louisville slugger.
& he put it in the trunk of his black sedan
& he got behind the wheel of his black sedan
& drove into the dreary heartland:
state welcome-signs whizzed by his head,
at the corner of his eyes
like so many Carl Mays pay-back pitches.
Night cold & dark as spilling shark gut
heavy with cuttlefish ink,
as far as the eye can see.

The baseball star ends up
in some part of the great prairie
gets out of the car,
his eyes sunken & purple, his jowls dangling,
& he walks into some earnest cornfield.

"It just takes one hit!" Babe yells
& starts swinging his stick into the tall corn.
From the left side, really letting loose;
in a whirlwind of intense power
he starts demolishing the field
whacking the corn into pulp / pig fodder,
mashing the green out of the leaves
sending the stalks into other counties.
"Fuck Iowa!" he says
"Fuck the cornfields, & the green blades of grass,
fuck the Mighty Casey & his Mudville saps,
fuck Frank Capra & the white sugar ulcer
given to me & this godamned game."
The John Deere combine of his swing,
the force of his grip turning his knuckles white,
& he finishes off the cornstalks
until the field is clear, good as plowed,
& Ruth just starts pounding into the earth /
& lumps of worm thick sod are uplifted
sent flying above & beyond
the smell of damp soil overwhelming,
like dark blood from a stomach wound.

& Babe starts burrowing downwards —
a mad miner on a strange mission —
he beats through roots, the layer of top soil,
rocks, clay, through Indian graves & solidified oil.
Through the earth's crust ultimately
just hitting, hitting with all the rage
his cancer had brought on, singing
"Tessie, Tessie, won't you come home."
Through the fossils, to a spot magma hot,
a cavern in the fold of the deep earth,
the hole in the ground that Ruth built.

& all of a sudden there's a bit of light,
a dim yellow porch stoop light
& there's a bucket of baseballs
each one grimed over with red Mississippi mud
& signed "A. Bartlett Giamatti."
So Babe does what comes natural,
one by one he flips the balls in the air
takes his primordial stick
& starts belting line drives,
& long roping loopers into the dark,
way past the confines of any fence
500, maybe 600 feet.
He never hears the balls land
or bounce off the cavern walls.
& George Herman Ruth,
the bad kid from Baltimore
the red, white & blue cigar-chomping
skirt-chasing, whisky-drinking,
ball-playing embodiment of a country's soul
kept merrily swatting away.
Crack! Crack! Crack!
The more he hit out into the hollow,
the more the flood lights would come on,
until he could see ominous red stalactites
ready to break & kill
& a yellow kitchen door flush
with the damp rock wall.

He finished with the bucket of balls,
a blood blister at the base of his right hand
& went & peered through the door's screen.
All he could see was a cool blue light flickering.
He banged on the aluminum
& said "anyone home?"

He opens the door, says it again inside
& somebody inside, a male voice, goes
"take off your shoes!
We just had the carpets done!"
Babe kicks off his loafers
& walks gingerly to where the voice
& the blue light are coming from.
His face is pale as mouse-fur
& he wears a wet, fake smile.
Through the hallway with prints of barns
& by a small bathroom with towels askew
he ends up at a living room
where a family is watching color TV.
They are watching a show
about a family just like them.
The mother says to the guest
"can I get you something?
Some slippers for your feet?"
The TV is bigger, nicer than anything
he has ever seen.
"Wow. This is a weird place.
For a second I thought I was in hell,
or at least some kind of purgatory."
& when the commericals are on, the father says
"well, it used to be something like that here
but y'know how complaisant
things have got. We can't be bothered."
All the ads are for self-improvement products:
whiter teeth, flatter stomach, bigger hair.
"Listen Jidge" the father whispers
not to disturb the family
"you're not out of the underworld yet."
But there would be no lip-smacking Cerberus,
no towers of white hot acetylene fires,

no cow gut spilling over the freshly whipped head
no visceral humiliation of the beast
that made its way through a human life.
After the show, an older man, maybe an uncle
takes Babe aside, lights a cigar
a Davidoff-Corona hand rolled in Cuba
& hands it to the Babe.
He says, like he has somewhere else to go
"Just through that door,
the one with
the stained-glass my niece designed,
just through that door you go
& there, all of a sudden, just like that
you will be in Ocean City Maryland 1991,
(how's that for purgatory?)
& you'll be on the beach
& you'll meet someone.
Her name is Kate, I think."
& Babe complimented him on the cigar
thinking again that this is really weird
this is just about the end
& the old man starts singing
"the people way down below
have gots a new m.o. . . . ."
& he wheels about, catches his breath
& tells Ruth where he is going:
a world full of oil spills, radon gas,
pcbs, fluorocarbons, $H_2S$, benzene,
& monoxide & acid rain.
& a nuclear build up to blast
all our little tales of way down there
& baseball into the cold lungless air of space.
Babe, then, just wants to go fast
to get out from below

into the dangerous place
to check out the woman behind the door;
he's heard it all before he says.
But before he heads out, he's stopped.
The old man says "if
you want to leave
you have to help us with this crossword"
& the uncle pulls out a tattered newspaper clip
squints & asks
"what's a 4 letter word for 'sultan's work'?"
"That's easy" Babe says
"Swat!"
& he pats the uncle on the back
& runs on his spindly legs
never looking back, out the door
to the beach beyond.

# The Trip

The trip was supposed to be simple enough:
drive Hank Williams from Knoxville TN to Canton OH,
give him time to dry out, straighten up
for a New Year's Eve concert the next night.
But I had to bring the car from Montgomery AL,
the first capital of that confederacy, 1861,
where Jim Crow ruled supreme as cotton, 1954,
& where blood was spilled not thirty years ago
for daring to cast a vote, sit anywhere on a bus.
I had to take the first cadillac cowboy's cadillac
all the way through the Smoky Mountains
& through a heavy wet snow
that grounded all the planes.

I was to take him wherever he wished.
& Ole Hank (he annoyingly referred to himself
in third person) wanted to go on
just another wild ride.
He needed some shots for the pain in his back
which was real at one time, but that day
he was riding the crest of a junkie's heat,
a hot spell that eats the user like a fever
from fix to fix until, someway, it dies down.
First business in Knoxville was to see
the doctor who would oblige Ole Hank.
Instead of starting north
we tooled around the south in the white caddy.
A dusty bottle of whisky from Fort Payne AL
was soon shattered, empty on the road. Then, then, then
we got to Chattanooga TN to see another doctor
another needle that I guess he couldn't
brave himself to spike.
Picked up some chloral hydrate tablets —

something to keep him from drinking
(you kept Hank from drinking by knocking him out).
The mountains were grey in the snow
but still missing the Christmas magic
Dolly Parton associates with the region.
Travelling through you could never tell
throughout the fields; stench
is left to fester on the battlefields;
gangrene, osteomyelitis, pyemia, peritonitis,
dysentery, typhoid, pneumonia, malaria
& of course just plain shot to death,
like Lincoln. Just passing through
you wouldn't know. God is silent that way.
Hank had a guitar back there
& now & then he'd manage a few stray strums,
or an out-of-tune chorus to "I saw the light."
The guitar was so big in his scrawny lap,
so sharp in its angles,
it looked like it might mangle him
like a big greasy machine.
I tended, even then, to be disgusted
by the extent of his illness,
his Jack Daniels emaciation,
where you could see too clearly
the bony machinations of the lower jaw,
& his teeth always exposed,
brown with tobacco tartar, his lips
deprived of any healthy puff of fat.
But it was true:
he could sing your ass off,
sing you to the very brink of the country western
understanding of the world.

He wasn't the first to burn out his or her star,
& he won't be the last. He had spina bifida
& a talent for expressing loneliness,
maybe more than anybody before.

& for the longest time those songs,
so plaintive yet so sweet, nestled
in the deepest parts of my day-to-day.
Made me afraid to reach out,
seized up my knees like an ill-advised surgery
that replaced slippery cartilage
with rusty sheet metal & pins.
"Are you OK, Mr. Williams?" I asked
& he cussed & took a slug & said
"Ole Hank's alright" & we slid along,
the cadillac smooth as a skiff in the bayou,
silent, watching the grey winter forests of Tennessee,
way into the southern ridge of the Appalachian plateau
over the muddy tributaries, catfish thick,
of the Mississippi & Ohio rivers.
Jesus was on my mind, his mercy
wouldn't bring us through the snowfall, would it?
Jesus wouldn't bring us through —
through to that place like heaven
& by dawn we were in Chattanooga & Hank
saw his man & limped into the car
with another head-full of bootsauce.
He is coming.
To Chattanooga where the rebels pitched well
but disastrously lost the battle of Chickamauga,
Yankees storming their position on Missionary Ridge,
chanting, Chickamauga! Chickamauga!
& Grant's men forced General Bragg into Georgia
Nov. 25 1863, demoralizing the CSA,
the blood of the young in the creeks,
smell of gunpowder in the fog, a huge
American flag raised at the top of the hill.
Yessir that doctor fixed Hank up pretty good
& gave me some little white things
that would keep me wide awake well into northern OH.
By the time we got back to where we started,
behind schedule,

already intolerably weary of driving,
the car stank of malt
& Hank needed more than a day to straighten up.
More than a decade.
I saw Knoxville again,
the first time I left my wife in 1984,
& it was incredible, host of the World's Fair,
& I took in the humidity like a tonic
& lay around drunk just about anywhere.
Knoxville too was occupied by Union troops
in the autumn of 1863 & they resisted
any & every attempt to oust them.
I asked Hank if he wanted to stop here,
pretend all the night was a dream
& start again fresh,
maybe drive into a snowbank for fun.
But he said no & made gestures with his hand
as if to say: not now, Ole Hank
is busy making music history.
"I will you you (sic) still & always will
but that's the poison we have to pay"
is what the wreck coughed out in the back,
his last contribution to the lyric.
Snow, let it, powerful, drop heavy.
From then on, he said, I was the boss
& let loose & drove North East
& we were pulled over by this Tennessee cop.

Who snarled at the room-sized sedan
"Hey, 'bama boy," he said, looking at my plates
"that's one lawwng car. Who's in back?"
That's all he wanted to know.
He was only there because of the snow
to watch traffic through the Virginia/Tennessee border
where, by the way, Ulysses S. Grant,
a reported boozehound & certain military victor himself,
seized the Virginia & Tennessee rail-lines

in the first serious offensives of 1864,
more dead, of course, both sides. Afternoon.
"Hey, if that guy is Hank Williams
that guy looks dead," the cop said
& caught some thick flakes in his meaty palm
& licked them like a clumsy bear cub.
& we drove on into the thick Allegheny forest,
into those beautiful blue pines, & mudslick hollers.
Into Bluefield VA, an unremarkable town,
except Mr. Williams had a doctor there
whom he said he'd like to see,
but passing through, Hank was passed out,
the choral nitrate, the whachamacallit I thought,
& stopped & had a sandwich by myself
dry roast beef, & a heart warming beer.

I had another & another until I was pestering
the waitress, saying, "didja know
Hank Williams is this big time Dodgers fan"
because the waitress admitted she liked Brooklyn too.
"& every year he gets choked when the NY Yankees
best them in the end, those Bums." Oh, O.
Hank never saw them play with Jackie Robinson
but he heard of him hustling out in AAA
for the Montreal Royals
at gentle Delormier fields not far from the
foot of the Jacques Cartier bridge.
In the end she wasn't impressed.
She turned off the grill.
Late night, had to travel slow through the snow,
Hank looked really bad.
We would never make the New Year's show.
I didn't want to find out.
I threw some take-out in the back seat,
a white paper bag that was never opened.
I thought I heard him stir when we started out
& if he had any life then

I'm sure he was thinking about the beer I bought,
the new life inside the long white cadillac.
I think it was full of song stuff.
I guess he didn't stir, passed through Princeton wv
& we were close to the limit of Confederate excursions.
West Virginia was quickly incorporated into the Union.
I was thinking we were just nitwits travelling
but 40 miles north I realized,
it was obvious, Hank Williams was dead.
Tony Bennett's version of "Cold Cold Heart"
would no longer rouse him to violence.
I stopped in Oak Hill wv to tell somebody
there was a dead man, cold, in my car, his car,
whatever. & they came & said I was right
Hiram Williams was dead at the age of 30.
Police headquarters, telephone calls.
Excessive eulogies flowed from then on,
from people who wouldn't shake a hand before
& who looked on while the last stage of illness set in.
"The Hillbilly Shakespeare" they said,
which is only as accurate or inaccurate
as calling the Bard the Renaissance Hank.
Schubert, it seems, is the logical parallel,
but it too doesn't matter, I'm tired
& I don't know what to say any more.
Oak Hill wv, hundreds of miles south,
(too late, anyway) from the Canton oh promised land.
Canton oh, site of the Pro Football Hall of Fame,
Mike Ditka's jersey there in a football-shaped building.
Just north of Salinville, the Northernmost point
of any rebel excursion: Greycoat cavalry raiders
under General Morgan surrendered there July 26 1863.
Although, once, St. Alban's vt was raided
by about 30 Confederates from their base in Canada.

# The Wreck of *The Atlantic*

*The Atlantic* was lost before the New Year
A Nova Scotian cargo ship, down on her luck,
Unable to tough out a fifty hour storm.
She was hauling a cache of stolen Japanese TVs
Picked up on the Carolina coast.
They were worth more than *The Atlantic* herself
Worth more than every bit that was dragged into the salter.
I made it out alive but still lack the poetry to tell it all.
Now the colors sit in me.
Editors and reviewers enjoy color:
I kick and scream
But it remains unmovable.
I say green like cheese, red like cheese
And fuschia, like
Cheese.

Mailed postcards home on Boxing Day;
"Sorry we're all so busy at Christmastime
Ordinarily I'd like to hear what you have to say."
Shoved off with a persistent feeling of doom.
Nothing new.
Used to writing terse suicide notes,
Leaving them in my mouth as I lay down,
Confident I'd eat the embarrassing words in my sleep.
Who knows why I joined this crew
And didn't end up stacking tins of motor oil at the new
        Wal-Mart.

Cpt. Harnett was from Saskatchewan.
There were scars about his face where melanomas
Were removed at the Royal Victoria Hospital in 1992.
Since then he had resolved to be more open,
Less of a policeman, less of a corpse.
Said there were things bigger than *The Atlantic*

Things bigger than the dogs' teeth he sees in his sleep.
"All the mountains, prairies, and towns
Can be removed to the sea
But it can not change my love."

The cook was less influenced by St Matthew.
He said "before I left for this trip
I sat at home with the TV Guide
I circled all the slots marked "to be announced"
And programmed them on my VCR
I wonder what kind of crap is waiting for me at home."
He agreed with the captain that in this world
There was no revenge, no comeuppance
Though he offended when he said
"There is no salvation, but there is soup.
Soup is all in the end.
It unites cultures, cures colds, it even comes in cans.
It may turn out that I wasn't the Cordon Blue-bound man
I thought I was in junior college
But I have no fear of soup
No fear of the potato-grief of the middle class.
Pie, on the other hand
Is something that fills me with dread.
So many beautiful slices look like porcelain,
Some even make you sick.
Pies are of the day,
Subject to the worst intentions."

There were the hands, the loser-men, the 4-eyes,
The fatsos, the mama's boys, the Mooses, the bookworms,
The wing-nuts, the preachers' sons, the boozehounds,
The country-boys, the clowns, the crooks, and the
        suspiciously quiet.
And there was me not doing much but hating my life,
Hating my looks, the whole teenage bit.

After sailing from Carolina, the TVs all tied on deck,
We turned our thoughts to Christmas now that we'd be
　　　getting paid.
Oh how we remembered those cherished times:
　　　the sloppy food,
The sight of our Mothers weeping because they had
"Tried so hard"; the phonecalls from strayed brothers
　　　and sisters;
The Hallmark moments when we looked at our fathers
　　　and asked
"Daddy, are you drunk?"

I wasn't sure what day it was
Or how many days to port
When the weather turned bad.
With the thunder and rain
*The Atlantic* could not fight the waves
The boat falling and smashing down
Like a mechanical hammer-press.
We puked and danced
As it began to *not stop*.
The Cpt. said they could do nothing
But ride the storm and pray.
We had never seen him pray
But imagined he knew how to do it right.

The cook said the kitchen had been destroyed
"And this is no time to fight a grease fire."
That was the first note to our night song:
*The Atlantic* was going down.
Apologies roared for forgiving wives,
For unathletic children,
For pissing away our God-given talent.
We were still looking to express our way out of it.
No videotape, please.
The radio made noise but we couldn't get a message.
We used every bit of tech knowledge,

Tried French, tried Spanish:
It was all gibberish.
We were going down all right
In the 39th hour of the storm
*The Atlantic* began to quiver like a compass needle
And we began to shake too
I didn't know if the buzz was worse in the ship
          or in my arms.
The lifeboats had been smashed.

The Cook and the Cpt. joined forces
They said something like
"Now that I can see, I will not return to the dark."
Still, they left us alone, sick and dumb,
Circling, circling.

I fell asleep as *The Atlantic* dropped into the deep.
Some of my teeth had been knocked out
And the salt ripped at my mouth.
All around the boxes with the stolen TVs
Popped up like mercenary dolphins.
Buoyant merchandise had finally
Saved my life.
I held onto that Japanese TV and kicked
Towards something, I couldn't really say what
Still couldn't feel past the rips in my throat.

# FOUR

# All the *thirtysomething* Characters Die

There is no more art in the furry mitted
stabs to reach the abyss
while living in the Northeast of America.
Sad to say, it's been done to death
& leaves us all dumb as anvils
waiting for the commuter in the snow.
Madison Ave. reports that in the 90's
what sells isn't sex or product performance
but bittersweet emotion.
All that endures toward the crucial synapses
that take place in supermarket aisles
is emotion. On the worst day of my life
I ate a sandwich, fries & ice cream.
Worried about our phone bill
& still yearning for a try despite
its artless hospital stays & early goodbyes.
No miraculous conversions,
no green antlers to sprout
just the porridge of no more.
The river takes them all,
all their bits, under the ice to a Delaware beach.

# Mike Seaver Dies

The glint is nowhere near the eyes
of the Seaver boy. Don't prolong the suffering.
Let each water drop fall, sparkle
& pass through the earth.
No iconoclastic brassiere straps
or corresponding imprints forever gouged
in some goosefleshy shoulder;
a memory wanting to be purple as wildflower
or an album cover. I don't know.
Fat sister falls through the roof,
Mother is tempted by teenage son's friend
but runs through the forest instead.
Can still smell the pine late at night
when her husband rolls this way then the next.
This is a flare gun pointed up to Cassiopeia
or a tapioca order at the K-Mart buffeteria.
Dead, dead: that is the part immutable.

# Cosby Kid Spasms

Before the doctor ever cut through towards my back,
to jam through my slipped disc like a stuck slug,
I told him & his nurse my million dollar idea:
Cosby kid cough-drops, relief in the face-shapes
of our favorite Huxtables: *Lemon Theo* for sore throats,
*Cherry Vanessa* for a runny nose, *Grape Rudy*
        for a dry cough
& *Menthol-Lyptus Denise* for all three. & the doctor laughed
in his warm southern methodist way & said
"Don't be disappointed if your surgery is rescheduled."
Disappointed? Through the hospital window I could see
nothing: no trees, no radio towers, no clouds, in any shape,
no larks, or streetlights. Nothing except the snappy
blue of a dry, cold December afternoon.
The nurse said: "Cosby would sue you to death,
here, take these" & she gave me more wonderful pills,
"they will momentarily confuse the devil in your spine."

# Master Po Turns His Back on Me

Master Po turns his back on me
the wave of his orange robes
makes the candles flicker,
their shadows like cock fights
before the feathers & blood.

I was not made for the Shaolin Temple.
When they would talk of tiger breath
or of losing yourself like a good bonfire
I dreamt of Nina Li Cheh
& took home a C+/B- kung fu grade,

Not bad but not the mark of a priest.
Master Po is in town by now
drinking Japanese beer & griping about the quitters.
It wasn't like that in the old days when students
knew Buddha mind like the back of their hand

"Kill a prince & fly to USA, grasshopper
It will appear as *incomplete* on your transcript."
My kicks can only go so far.
The candles burn bright again.
They tear out my eyes.

# Oprah State University: The First Valedictory Address

This summer I will swim Lake Michigan.
Not in width or length
but I promise I'll get in it for awhile.

I had parents no better than algae
or at least no better than walleyes,
their eyes cloudy, their gills full of ash, though still alive.

But they did tell me to go to college
and told me to keep a 9mm pistol in my desk
and I do, just to keep my inner child alive.

Now as we head out into the world
I can look an employer square and say
don't believe *The Enquirer*, feel good about yourself!

Next fall, I will sit down
in my XXL OSU sweats
and laugh at all the ridiculous headlines.

As an adult graduate of a co-dependent academy
I will do my best to sign a letter
that may close down a radio station in Maine.

I will moonwalk to principal Graham's office
to tell him, for all the children, on the eve of morning
of seizing a momentous North American — something.

I will, at least, run down Michigan avenue
a Coney dog in each hand;
just running and biting, biting and running.

# George Bush Has Retired To My Back Yard

For more than 3 years now in the same lower duplex
where every summer we ask each other
what do you call the blossoms that sour the air
and crumble the day after they bloom.
Now, I don't want to know —
I was happier when I thought Venus was just a star,
happier before we were engaged in a war
          with the upper duplex —
too sensitive to noise.

This summer George Bush has been doing the yard.
He is very good. Once it's done, out come the sticks
sometimes he putts, sometimes he chips.
We think of inviting him to a barbecue
but usually forget. Once I swear I heard him mutter
"that idiot Bob Teeter" and when I said "what was that?"
he said "I said I think I need a weed whacker . . .
that would be best for this here garden, fella."

For more than 3 years now in the same lease.
We used to move from Vermont to Boca Raton to St. Paul
just like that. We would watch the fields from the car:
each stretch tantalizingly different,
reassuringly the same.
Summer waffles the outlook; we become a plot
out of *Roseanne*. Poppy mows and putters
in the back 4 we rent, with no plan to own.

# Stedmanland

I've come to the Big Island to fulfil a dream.
Anything to escape my nightmares (my looks)
anything to miscue the lenses of helicopter cameras,
lead them into the landscape of Hawaii
into the volcanic outgrowth they mistake as exotic,
and enshrine in tiki-rooms from Maine to Saskatoon.
I've come to paradise to build a funland.
A theme-park with one theme in mind:
*do not remind me of the past.*

There's a mysterious virus in my neck.
It has made me see blue;
has given me insight into what they're saying
behind my back.
When they say "he's a nice guy,"
I understand that they're after my money.
I'm no Kamehameha, no Keanu Reeves
but my plaguey stump still holds a Christian head.
I have time to tape, watch, rewind, rerecord;
I have time to embrace my back.
O money (not mine) endless as the Pacific,
sultry as green fire,
and tear-away like pig-meat.
Celebrate the dysfunction, darling;
let Piebald Jackson take care of the view.
I can see into the coffee or pineapple hills —
the point is: *Hawaii USA.*

I live with the neck thing.
It doesn't feel like the blade of the mirror,
it doesn't put me off my poi.
Beyond the orchids, the waterfalls,
I wait and plan my horizon's glow.
I make jokes about the voters on Oahu
and dream of Stedmanland.
The I'm-Not-Gay Funhouse,
Wedding-Cancellation Mountain
and, of course, the Oprahcoaster.

Tabu is a word my lawyer understands.
He is across that pearl,
and God can forgive me if he must.

# Kentucky Fried Dublin

Hungry, due to see a curious
*Plough & the Stars*
we loaded down on the Colonel's extra-crispy.
Sopped up the gravy à la Elvis on a binge:
"Extra, uh, tea biscuits, ma'am."
Later, at a touristy pub,
a young man with a limp asked me
if I knew that Dublin's KFC
was voted the best KFC in Europe.
I had no idea they had elections,
but told him a story of somebody
who once met Colonel Sanders himself.

It was a warm summer in Ireland,
conversation half-hearted & transparent;
hashing over moments from *Simpsons* episodes,
& fearing the threat of tainted meat.
The Kentucky-fried made the play too long:
crazed with protein, it was hard to concentrate.

That night in Dublin I saw more people
vomit in the street than I ever thought possible;
more than in Times Square on New Year's Eve
more than Times Square on St. Patrick's Day.
I told the guy with the limp, in Canada
there was no extra-crispy or tea biscuits
so that at least in chicken-frying technology
the Republic was well ahead;
by then he was pretty much fed up with my accent.
Pint gulps, MC Hammer's "Can't Touch This"
a Eurail pass in my pants pocket & a hotel key,
its key chain tab large as a slice of bread
close to my side.

# FIVE

# Porkscraps

He hit me over the head with a shovel
made of soft plastic but I deserved it.
And that, apparently, wasn't enough
I rewrote *The Barkleys of Broadway*

As *Those Magnificent Malignancies*
and got laughed the fuck out of Manhattan.
Oooh ouch I said all the time like a dolt —
I wasn't supposed to be exerting myself.

I wasn't even supposed to mention the weather
to a certain shovel-wielding neighbor;
the big-city guy who looks like Stalin
and claims he's acted with *the* Traci Lords.

"Here's a Tony award for you" he said
before he crowned me the king of New York
and I collapsed in the brown salty snow
just thinking *I really did it this time.*

# Margarine Sunshine

The replacement ballplayers scratched like pros
and I lined-up to get me an autograph,
get one to initial a liver spot or phone my kid —
"tell him that you're that fat guy with the Detroits."

Getting all angry drunk under the sun,
I got into the worst kind of trouble
arrested for "mascot molestation"
I was called a "sicko" by a *sportswriter*.

I tried to phone home to arrange bail.
I couldn't get through, (although a sexy voice
told me all about how to "save on long-distance calls")
and I had a rash from polyester mascot-fur.

My lawyer said it was old hat to him
he had covered several cases in Philly
involving that big stupid green thing.
He said: 1-800-GO-RICKI

# Tubby's T.O.

My cinnamon-toast swoosie
my cancerous lambada dilly
my limpid dropover klatch
is all as good as it gets.

(For legal reasons) I cannot say
why it's corked-up like this;
I have a friend, a male model PhD,
who just says "ip dip dee dee"

In the T.O. waterways I swim like an otter
and nearly as cute, I nibble
at the edges of everything I see.
(and blame any sour taste on plastic habitat)

*Is that all you thought of this week?*
I shouldn't think of the wee endangered?
*Don't you want to get better?*
I want that job folding sweaters.

# Double-Butterfat Lardcake

I knew by the way the letter began
("Dear Snotty") that today wasn't my day.
But still, I managed my way to the workplace
and threw-up gently in the wastebasket.

My colleagues acted like I was making tea
and said with their eyes (and in other words)
that they will not get involved in my life
until *Hard Copy* offers them some cash.

I write mad notes in the margins of reports
and mope about a look I doubt I ever had;
was there really a Golden Age, unseen
like the cinema of Zsa Zsa Gabor?

The letter smelled like an old turtle tank
and the words grew markedly unpleasant
and pompous: did she think it was the first time
the word "lardassed" had been used on me?

# Grey Gravy-Boy

I had a dream about Hillary.
She told me I was just like a Mormon,
except without the family values
and the exquisite orthodontery.

I woke up and wrote to the President,
using fancy words as I often do.
The next thing I knew I was on the ground
while secret service men went hee hee.

Sent upstate to serve out a nickel
I told the shrink it was all a good thing —
Thank God I didn't dream of Charles Barkley —
just let me rot or rehabilitate.

Now I have a pumpkin-sized prostate
and I sing like a loon full of bad bear-meat
up and down everynight, smacking my head
into the facilities, like *thwack thwack*

# Pudgy *Pathetique*

When I delude myself that I'll publish
before the beer has liquified my brain
and that my quirky books will be displayed
in hip bookstore windows up on the Main

I conjure up new ways to say taco
and dive, belly first, into the muddy:
teeco, twaco, here I go; Delmore, Delmore
I'll never go and be that lovely.

I sit in the deep hearts of e-z chairs
and have given my M.A. to my thumb:
I'm not any happier this way but
at least I don't have to answer the phone.

I sit in fear of another attack
heart or panic, I'm unable to choose.
Stalled in the face of what should be well-done
at least I know the end should rhyme with booze.

# Fatso Fidelio

In the Marcia Brady Wing of the library today
I wondered if I could coax Jan to smile.
I didn't really have a joke worked out
except the no longer funny "I have it licked."

So I looked through books about pie-stealing saints
and things even Jan could sarcastically umpire over.
But by that time she was gone, ungrateful middlechild,
unaware that we could make a soup in vain.

Failure soup is different than failure stew
but I assure you it's the greater failure of the two.
In a place called Nova Scotia I tried the chowder
and I read that I'm lucky to be alive.

Did you hear that, Jan? *I wasn't trying anything.*
It was just a little extra homework
towards our honorary PhDs — don't you ever
think of the gowns they'd make us wear?

# Scrapplicious

I phoned an old professor of mine
to brag of my soon-to-be-published verse
"let me switch ears" he said, "another poem
about barfing at the auto show?"

Chastened, I switched subjects and dropped my voice
and began listing the names of people I could beat up,
whose faces would disappear on a fist,
"is this a poem?" he said before hanging up.

Another letter of recommendation lost
another wise man who has stopped laughing.
Is this about the weight? Is it too late?
Do I sound too much like Bobcat Goldthwait?

Firecracker sounds make me sleepy now
and I'm sure I'll sell all my Yeats at the yard sale
because it's all true you know
(except for the soon-to-be-published part)

# Bubba Jive

Just after the doctors
declared me parasite-free,
you come into my life
looking like a million popsicles.

And you have your own s & l
with murals of Lincoln's teen years in Indiana
in the lobby; in the kitchenette
a little place to put your shoes.

I remember because
that is where I went I don't
and made some comment about blonde hair
which isn't as dull as my daily.

You wouldn't know it by my suit
but God is out to get me,
you can see that in my face — you see —
you don't have to say anything, darlin

# Jumbo's Ju-Ju

This is as close as I'll get to MTV
to boxer or brief you;
to shout out to all those little parents
I once called my own.

It's percodan-errific
the way you erase my years;
you are the wind shear
beneath my wings.

Gone the way of all Dans and Daves
straight to the prelims to do something *weird*
and then to blame the performance on you
apple fresh and near enough.

I can't believe it's not prozac
the way I dream of you
and your bus-pass scowl,
breaking stuff over my head.

# Lemon Pudge

The white mice have pretty much taken over
I don't care if I see them on the counter
I'm just worried I'll step on one
and it'll squeak "narcissist" as it fades.

That's pretty much the life story
at least since the winter-college dream
of marrying riches with my hair and art
took a job with a national chain.

An office romance developed in time;
Polyester on polyester — *oowee*
I was too embarrassed to have her over
so I called the thing off and put out the traps.

Good enough: she really wanted kids
because she can't wait to tell them
what shows they're not allowed to watch
and how much they'll regret giving up piano.

# Los Lardos

This is our tacoghetti night out
bumping into walls saying
"do you remember how to pronounce Montreal?"
Magnasomething, I suppose.

Things on my skin suddenly
on a first name basis in a California clinic
that does not use the words.
*Canceroso; dermatological neoplasm.*

The Lardos take the stage
and do their midnight shinola
cold Budwinky in my hand
and the Spanish words to English songs.

Can you guys play *Old Angus the Chimp*?
And they don't even call security
no matter: I'm lost in the taxi
all those directions, this breath.

# KoKo

There was no doubt about my boss:
he was one of the great defectives.
He claimed our poor profits in the recession
stemmed from his "fear of circus clowns."

You have to be careful around a guy like that:
test your breath, shoelaces Oxford-style —
one winter afternoon, about a month
after the operation on my foot,

I limped aggressively into the office
and *finally* told a co-worker to shutup.
My boss overheard, grabbed me and said,
"you're not the sharpest pencil in the box, are you?"

The irony was I ended up working as a clown
in front of a flower shop right there on 6th avenue.
And the boss would walk by, smelling like *Paco Rabanne*
and I was going shutup, shutup, shutup.

# Gasbaggie

Jimmy Carter accidentally nailed
my foot to a screen door
so I'll be damned if I think of him as under-rated
as the infection I had was severe and now I walk funny.

But I don't walk much anyway
I carry a mattress out to the living room
and just lie there my eyes fixed to the blue
because I can't miss the fashion shows.

In the future, supermodels
will get Congress to enact laws of "positivity"
because when I say negative things about my looks,
it makes *them* feel really bad.

Even the nurses didn't want to hear it because
my foot, in a strange way, was *famous*
got more coverage than many fine independent films
and why should I feel sorry for you?

# Chunk

If you'll be my darling
I'll be your Mayor McCheese,
in the morning we'll get in the car
and start tilting down the street.

When I'm asleep at the wheel
I'll mumble of my personal hell —
hell, I'll be your Brian Krakow
if you can do something about the smell.

In the afternoon I'll get stitches
that'll scar out three little words all black and blue
and I'll let you use my insurance
floridly signed Mr. & Mrs. Magoo.

Because it's burgertime *ce soir*
*ma 'tite fille de la belle Ville D'Anjou*
Oh, I'll be your Billy Ray Cyrus
if that means anything to you.

# O Coconut

I live in that part of Canada
where people eat a quart of bologna everyday
and call each other names like "Debbie" or "Bill"
but they don't really mean it.

The lap dances are just fine
so it's the weather that gets you down.
Once, the snow was so deep
you almost couldn't hear Margaret Atwood.

We boast about the politeness.
And it's all very true: whenever I return videos
the clerks always take the time to say
"thank you, pervert."

*It isn't so bad* is just the kind of thing we say
because it's not like we don't have daiquiris
and can't remember the bad old days
when our problems were mostly odor-related.